Isabel's
House of Butterflies

by Tony Johnston

illustrated by Susan Guevara

 SRA

Columbus, OH

Reprinted by permission of Sierra Club Books for Children.

SRAonline.com

McGraw Hill **SRA**

Printed in Mexico.

Send all inquiries to:
SRA/McGraw-Hill
4400 Easton Commons
Columbus, OH 43219-6188

ISBN 978-0-07-612513-5
MHID 0-07-612513-0

2 3 4 5 6 7 RRM 13 12 11 10 09

The **McGraw·Hill** Companies

*For the Camporredondo family
and for Hans Gysin,* El Estimado,
*companion on so many trips
through Mexico,* lindo y querido
—T.J.

*For Antonio Hernández Madrigal
and* mi hermana loca, *Betsy James*
—S.G.

Deep in the forests of Michoacán, Mexico, in
an area about 300 miles square, is a natural
sanctuary for monarch butterflies.

Once in secret, but now more openly, loggers
are felling these forests. On a smaller scale, people
living in deep poverty here sometimes chop down
a butterfly tree to sell the wood—to survive.

With new laws, the government is trying to stop
this destruction, but it is hard to do.

If these trees disappear, perhaps the monarchs
will find other trees. Or perhaps they will disappear, too.
Either way, the people here will lose this wonder.

—T.J.

I am Isabel. I am eight. And I have my very own tree. An *oyamel.* It grows outside the window, like a green church touching the sky. I call it *La casa de las mariposas,* The House of Butterflies.

Where I live, in Mexico, in the mountains, many *oyameles*
grow. Sometimes, when people are hungry, they chop them down
to sell the wood. But we could never do that. In autumn,
butterflies come to roost in my tree.

Papa says when it gets cold in the North, they fly a long way
to find a warmer place. Over mountains, over rivers, over fields
they fly. They have no map. But they know where to go.

Then Mama's eyes shine with tears. "*Es un milagro*" Mama says.
She thinks it's a miracle, how they always return to *La casa
de las mariposas.*

Now it is autumn again. The butterflies are back.
So many we cannot count them, not all of us together.

Before, the sky was blue. Now it's orange with wings.
Before, the path was just dust. Now it's an orange river.
There is no place to walk. So we must step on butterflies.
Butterflies step on us, too. They step on everything —
even our pigs.

Before, my tree was empty. Now not one branch
shows. *La casa de las mariposas* is nothing but
butterflies! I'm so happy, I feel as light as a butterfly.
I dance as if I am.

Our house has one big room for everything, where we
eat and play and sleep. Each day, while I sweep our room,
I look out the window at my tree to see the butterflies.
While mama and I pat tortillas, side by side, I forget to pat.
I look at my tree.

    "*Isabelita*," Mama reminds me, "*las tortillas*." But I hear
a smile in her voice.

    I'm not the only one who loves the butterflies.
Sometimes Mama also stops patting. Then I say,
"*Las tortillas, Mami.*" I smile for real.
And she laughs.

Sometimes I see our neighbors looking at my tree. They love the butterflies, I think. Even our pigs lying in the cool dust under the porch, love the butterflies. They love to eat them — as many as they can.

Sometimes on his way to weed his plot of beans, Papa gazes at my tree. He loves it too. And he is grateful for the tourists it brings.

"Tourists mean a little money," he says, "so perhaps we can get by."

All years are hard. But this one is mean. The rain has
not rained as before. The beans are few. The ears of corn,
stubby and small.

"*Es un tigre*," says Papa. A tiger of a year.

One day Papa herds the pigs into the village. To sell. The pigs don't want to move. They are happy eating butterflies in the yard. Still, they go, all snuffle and grunt. Big warm boulders, churning the dust, shouldering each other along.

The dry weeks pass. At night, Papa and Mama start whispering. Like dry grass. They sound worried.

"Money is scarce, *mi vida*," Papa says. "The pig money will not last long. Tourist tips are not enough. We must eat. What else can I do?"

"Not the tree . . ." Mama's voice trails off.

What do they mean? I wonder. I am worried too. And restless. Night after night, they whisper. Night after night, I flop on my *petate* like a broken butterfly.

One morning, at first light, I see something gleam in our room. I squint my eyes. It's Papa's machete, as bright as a slice of moon. Slowly, he turns it in his hands. Then he speaks softly. He sounds sad.

"It hurts my heart," he tells Mama. "*Me duele el corazón*. But I must cut down *Las casa de las mariposas*. I must sell the wood."

"No!" A voice splits the stillness like a machete blow. It is mine. "Find another tree!"

"The others are far away," says Papa. "They do not belong to me."

I am crying. Choking with tears. Sobbing, "No! No! No!" We are all sobbing then.

Papa says, *"Isabelita,* I love this tree. But I love my family more. We cannot eat butterflies."

I close my eyes, hoping this is a dream. In my head I hear a machete ring. I see a tree — a big tree full of butterflies — falling.

I go outside and sit on the butterfly path. I look up at *La casa de las mariposas*.

The sun is higher now. Already, Mama is on the porch patting tortillas, making a slappy kind of music. Slowly, the shadowy curtains of sleeping butterflies catch the light. They shine in bright orange flashes, like a flickering fire. As the sun warms them, they flutter to life again.

Then I feel something on my arm. Soft. So soft. A butterfly. Resting on me, pumping its wings.

Pump. Pump. I think of butterflies. Slap. Slap. I think of tortillas. I think of tourists too. As light as wings, an idea floats into my mind.

"*¡Mami! ¡Papi!*" I shout. "*¡Ya sé! ¡Ya sé qué hacer!*"
My words pour out like a stream of butterflies.

"Papa will bring the tourists, like always. Then
you and I, *Mami*, you and I will set up a small stand,
un puesito, by my tree. We will pat tortillas, side by side.
We will shape them with wings and toast them on the
comal. We will sell butterflies, *Mami*, and we will make
money too!"

Mama and I make *masa*, corn dough for tortillas.
Lumps of *masa* lie on the table in piles, like small hills.
Where we work, the air smells sweet. Sweet with corn.

Now we pat tortillas, side by side. But I forget to pat.
I watch the path.

"*Isabelita*," Mama reminds me, "*las tortillas*." She hugs
me. She smells like sweet corn too.

While I work I am not looking at butterflies. I am
looking for tourists. Hungry ones. I hope that many will
visit my tree. I hope they will buy many butterfly tortillas.
Then maybe Papa will not have to cut down *La casa
de las mariposas*.

My heart flutters, I am so excited. And scared.
I look down the path, I hold my breath, and I hope.